The Grace of God
Why We Need It
Bisi Oladipupo

Springs of life publishing

Contents

To Jesus Christ my Lord and Saviour; to Him alone that laid down His life that I might have life eternal. To Him that led captivity captive and gave gifts unto men (Ephesians 4; 8). One of those gifts is writing!

Bisi Oladipupo

Foreword

S o, why grace?

The word 'grace' is found one hundred and twenty-two times in the New Testament. Could there be a reason this word is so rampant in our new covenant?

Did you know that our salvation came by grace? (Titus 2:11).

Did you know that this Christian life is a life of grace?

Many of us are aware of the final benediction prayer that many pray after meeting: *"The grace of our Lord Jesus Christ, the love of God, and the fellowship of the Holy Spirit, be with us now and forever more."*

As Christians, our knowledge of grace must go beyond these words.

Most of the epistles in the New Testament start with "Grace be with you" (2 John 1:3; Philippians 1:2), and many also end with "Grace be to you" (Ephesians 6:24; Philippians 4:23).

This shows how much grace is needed in our Christian walk.

BISI OLADIPUPO

We are told to grow in grace (2 Peter 3:18) and be strong in the grace that is in the Lord Jesus Christ (2 Timothy 2:1).

This book will look at what grace is and how we need to walk in grace in our Christian walk.

Be blessed!

Bisi

Chapter 1
What is Grace?

G race is God's enabling power, and it is a gift.

We can see the definition of grace reflected in these scriptures:

"But by the grace of God I am what I am, and His grace toward me was not in vain; but I labored more abundantly than they all, yet not I, but the grace of God which was with me" (1 Corinthians 15:10).

We can see from this scripture that it was God's grace that allowed Paul to labour more abundantly than others. He clearly stated here that it was not him but the grace of God that was with him.

"Concerning this thing I pleaded with the Lord three times that it might depart from me. ⁹ And He said to me, "My grace is sufficient for you, for My strength is made perfect in weakness." Therefore, most gladly I will rather boast in my infirmities, that the power of Christ may rest upon me" (2 Corinthians 12:8-9).

Paul here was pleading with the Lord to take a trial away from him. The Lord responded that His grace was sufficient for Paul. Paul then said he would gladly boast in his infirmities that the power of Christ may rest upon him. In other words, God's enabling power would help him.

"For by grace you have been saved through faith, and that not of yourselves; it is the gift of God, [9] not of works, lest anyone should boast" (Ephesians 2:8-9).

We can see from this scripture that grace is a gift.

This scripture below speaks about Jesus Christ, our Lord and Saviour.

"And the Child grew and became strong [k] in spirit, filled with wisdom; and the grace of God was upon Him" (Luke 1:40).

If Jesus Christ needed the grace of God, then we sure need God's grace. We are not supposed to live our lives in our own strength but by the grace of God.

The good news is that grace has already been made available to us.

The scriptures tell us in the Book of John: *"And of His fullness we have all received, and grace for grace. [17] For the law was given through Moses, but grace and truth came through Jesus Christ"* (John 1:16-17).

Have you ever wondered what one of the main differences between the Old and New Testaments is?

The Old Covenant people had law but no grace. It was Jesus Christ who brought us grace. Therefore, we have a much higher standard than the people of the Old Testament because we have God's grace at work in us for those who yield to His grace.

In light of that statement, this scripture will shed more light: *"For sin shall not have dominion over you, for you are not under law but under grace"* (Romans 6:14).

We don't need to struggle; grace is available to us (John 1:16).

The Word of God is referred to as the "Word of His grace" (Acts 20:32), and Jesus Christ is the Word of God, full of grace and truth (John 1:14).

In other words, God's word has grace impeded in it so that we can obey and live it out, as His word is full of grace.

So, how do we receive grace? Let us have a look at this.

Chapter 2
How to Receive Grace

S o, how do we receive grace?

Grace and truth came through Jesus Christ (John 1:17); therefore, everything that Jesus Christ paid the price for is available to us by grace through faith.

In other words, everything we require is available by the grace of God, but we access this grace by faith.

The Lord has made His grace available to us. We just have to access it by faith.

"For by grace you have been saved through faith, and that not of yourselves; it is the gift of God, ⁹ not of works, lest anyone should boast" (Ephesians 2:8-9).

So, we are saved by grace through faith. We cannot save ourselves; Jesus Christ did this for us. All we have to do is access this by faith. We simply need to confess Jesus Christ as our Lord and Saviour, and we shall be saved.

"that if you confess with your mouth the Lord Jesus and believe in your heart that God has raised Him from the dead, you will be saved" (Romans 10:9).

This is how we access the grace for salvation that has already been provided for us by Jesus Christ, our Lord.

"As you therefore have received Christ Jesus the Lord, so walk in Him" (Colossians 2:6).

We receive grace by faith in accepting Jesus Christ, and we need to continue our walk in Him by grace through faith.

We also receive grace by acknowledging our weaknesses and asking for grace. We can see this in the Book of 2 Corinthians 12:8, when Paul went through trials and asked the Lord to take them away. The Lord told him that His grace was sufficient for him.

"Concerning this thing I pleaded with the Lord three times that it might depart from me. ⁹ And He said to me, "My grace is sufficient for you, for My strength is made perfect in weakness." Therefore most gladly I will rather boast in my infirmities, that the power of Christ may rest upon me" (2 Corinthians 12:9).

So, when we are weak, we can ask for grace, and the Lord will grant it to us, and we will be able to operate in His strength.

I remember a family member sharing a testimony. He was in Kenya and had travelled many hours that day. As he arrived, he thought he would get some sleep after many hours of travel by air and on the road to reach the destination.

As he arrived, he was told that he was going to minister. He said, "*Okay, just give me a few minutes.*"

The hall was packed, and everyone was waiting for the "man of God" to come and minister. He said that he was so tired, but he honoured the preparations of the people and went ahead to minister.

He shared that it was the most powerful ministration he had ever had up to that point. The gifts of the Spirit moved as people were delivered and set free. He said it definitely was not him; God's strength was made perfect in his weakness.

One requirement we can see very clearly in Scripture that allows more grace to operate and flow in our lives is humility.

"But He gives more grace. Therefore He says:

"God resists the proud, But gives grace to the humble" (James 4:6).

From the above scripture, it is safe to say that the life of a prideful person is very likely to be hard because God resists them. That is a hard statement, but it is scripture. God gives grace to the humble.

Therefore, our attitudes will determine whether or not we have more or less grace in our lives.

Why would anyone want to struggle in their own strength when grace is available? Why would anyone despise God's ability that will make things easier?

Since humility attracts grace, we need to know what humility is.

The Bible tells us that Jesus was meek and humble in heart (Matthew 11:29; AMP). Could this be why the grace of God was upon Jesus Christ (Luke 2:40)?

So, what is humility?

To have a good definition of what humility is, let us look at Scripture, where this word was used. We will then learn from the content of the account, which will tell us what humility really is.

One expression of humility is recognising that we have done wrong and repenting accordingly.

The Scripture tells us that Ahab was a very wicked king (1 Kings 21:25). However, when the Lord sent Elijah to warn him, he humbled himself, and the Lord showed him mercy.

"Seest thou how Ahab humbleth himself before me? because he humbleth himself before me, I will not bring the evil in his days: but in his son's days will I bring the evil upon his house" (1 Kings 21:29; KJV).

Note that Ahab humbled himself not before men but before God. One characteristic of humility is owning up: *"I missed it. l repent; Lord, please forgive me"*. No excuses, no blames, only simply admitting that we were wrong.

7

Let us have a look at another definition of humility from a scripture in the Book of Philippians:

"Let this mind be in you, which was also in Christ Jesus:

⁶ Who, being in the form of God, thought it not robbery to be equal with God:

⁷ But made himself of no reputation, and took upon him the form of a servant, and was made in the likeness of men:

⁸ And being found in fashion as a man, he humbled himself, and became obedient unto death, even the death of the cross.

⁹ Wherefore God also hath highly exalted him, and given him a name which is above every name" (Philippians 2:5-9; KJV).

Looking at this scripture, Jesus Christ, our Lord and Saviour, showed us the ultimate example of what humility is. Some people would refuse to drive through a certain neighbourhood just because it is run down.

When we have an assignment from the Lord, we must be prepared to adjust and do it at whatever cost. Jesus Christ is part of the godhead (Colossians 2:9), and our Lord and Saviour humbled Himself, and became a man, and remained obedient even unto death.

Therefore, it is safe to say that humility is laying aside our own agenda, forgetting about our physical status, and doing what the Lord tells us to do. If Jesus Christ, our Lord and Saviour, could become a man for us, what price is too much to pay?

The Scripture tells us that before honour is humility (Proverbs 18:12). The Bible also tells us to put on humbleness of mind (Colossians 3:12). If we don't pass our humility test, we may find ourselves circling the same issue repeatedly.

Is there anything that the Lord wants you to do that you are struggling with? Could the answer be "humility"? Humility is obeying the Lord at all times and seeing nothing as "how can I do that"? That could be pride.

The humble get grace. Once again, the Scripture tells us that *"and the grace of God was upon him"* (Luke 2:40). When we obey the Lord, we get grace.

We receive grace by humbling ourselves:

"Humble yourselves therefore under the mighty hand of God, that he may exalt you in due time:" (1 Peter 5:6).

We also receive grace by simply asking for it. Whatever area of life we are struggling in, we can ask for grace.

"Let us therefore come boldly unto the throne of grace, that we may obtain mercy, and find grace to help in time of need" (Hebrews 4:16).

Chapter 3
What Do We Need Grace For?

O ur salvation is actually by grace through faith (Ephesians 2:8). The Scripture also tells us that as we have received the Lord Jesus Christ, so should we walk in Him (Colossians 2:6). Therefore, as we have started this journey by grace, we do need grace to continue through faith. The faith part is just acknowledging the grace and activating it through faith. In other words, just taking steps appropriate to the grace we require.

So, what do we need grace for? We will go through Scripture to see where grace was applied to our Christian experience in the Lord.

Grace is required for ministry

This is why we need to know the grace of God upon our lives and stay within our grace.

Several years ago, a friend of mine was made a pastor in her local assembly. Because she was not a pastor by calling, she struggled in the position. She would get home and think about all the challenges members had shared with her. She found it overwhelming, and one day, she decided to step down from the position.

So, was there anything wrong with this sister? No, not at all. She was simply not called to the office of a pastor. Therefore, she had no grace for it. Grace comes from the Lord.

"Let every man abide in the same calling wherein he was called" (1 Corinthians 7:20; KJV).

Every office and calling requires grace. A pastor oversees people. He/she is not a guest minister where they give the message and move to another location. Pastors stay with the flock, and dealing with people can be challenging sometimes. Everyone is still on a journey of growth, and pastors have to deal with everyone at their point of growth. In addition to that, pastors have to counsel people, pray for others, ask after their welfare, and the list goes on. This is an office that requires grace, just like any other calling or office does.

Paul, who wrote most of the New Testament, put it this way:

*"But by the grace of God I am what I am, and His grace toward me was not in vain; but I labored more abundantly than they all, yet not I, **but the grace of God which was with me**"* (1 Corinthians 7:20).

Paul here acknowledged that it was the grace of God that helped him labour more abundantly than others. Hence, we need God's grace in ministry.

We operate our ministry and callings through grace. Paul ministered by grace:

*"**For I say, through the grace given to me**, to everyone who is among you, not to think of himself more highly than he ought to think, but to think soberly, as God has dealt to each one a measure of faith"* (Romans 12:3).

Every one of us is in ministry, not just those who stand behind pulpits on a Sunday morning. According to Scripture, we have all been given giftings and callings according to the gift of the measure of Christ.

"But to each one of us grace was given according to the measure of Christ's gift. 8 Therefore He says:

"When He ascended on high, He led captivity captive, And gave gifts to men" (Ephesians 4:7-8).

The Scripture also tells us: *"As every man hath received the gift, even so minister the same one to another, as good stewards of the manifold grace of God"* (1 Peter 4:10). We can see here that our giftings are expressions of the manifold grace of God.

Do you find it easy to do something that others struggle to do? Could this be an expression of the grace of God? Did you know that someone is waiting to be a beneficiary of that grace upon your life?

And while we are still speaking about grace in ministry, we do need to perceive the grace that others have. In Scripture, we can see a practical application of this. Paul was speaking in the Book of Galatians about how James, Cephas, and John perceived the grace given to him to minister to the heathen (Galatians 2:9).

When we know the grace of God on others, we will not place unnecessary demands on them. We will also know who to approach each time we require something, depending on the grace we need to tap into at that time.

We need grace to share the gospel

The scriptures tell us that great grace was upon the apostles who bore witness of the resurrection of Jesus Christ.

"And with great power the apostles gave witness to the resurrection of the Lord Jesus. And great grace was upon them all" (Acts 4:33).

Have you struggled to share your faith with others? Then perhaps it is time to step out of your own strength and ability and ask for grace.

We believe through grace

Our God has made everything available for us to believe. The Lord has even given us grace to believe. This grace is activated by faith.

"And when he was disposed to pass into Achaia, the brethren wrote, exhorting the disciples to receive him: who, when he was come, helped them much which had believed through grace" (Acts 18:27).

This tells us that everyone can believe, the grace is already available.

"For the grace of God that brings salvation has appeared to all men" (Titus 2:11).

Our Salvation is by grace

This point appears to look like the point we just mentioned, but there is a difference. Our salvation is by the grace of God (Acts 15:11; Romans 4:3-4), and it is received by grace through faith.

We are justified by faith, and we access this grace by faith (Romans 5:1-2).

This is why the scriptures tell us not to boast, as it is the gift of God.

"8 For by grace you have been saved through faith, and that not of yourselves; it is the gift of God, 9 not of works, lest anyone should boast" (Ephesians 2:8-9).

We release the grace of God for salvation when we accept it by faith, and this is how grace works in our lives in other areas.

Have you ever heard the word "remnant"? Did you know that it is all by the grace of God (Romans 11:5-7)? God is no respecter of persons; we simply access the grace already available by faith.

Grace is the remedy for sin

Under the Old Covenant, they had to obey laws, but there was no grace. Grace and truth came through Jesus Christ.

The remedy for sin is not to try harder, but simply to walk in the Spirit and acknowledge that we are now dead to sin (Romans 6:11; 1 Peter

2:24). The Scripture tells us that sin shall not have dominion over us because we are not under the law but under grace (Romans 6:14).

Are you struggling with any form of sin in your life? Then according to this scripture, you are dead to sin. Acknowledge the truth that we now have in Christ and ask the Lord for grace to overcome whatever you are dealing with in the flesh. You then need to yield to that grace by faith and follow any instructions that the Lord gives you.

Jesus paid the price for sin, and sin shall not have dominion over us.

We need grace when we go through tough times

This was made clear when Paul was going through a challenging time and the Lord told Paul, *"My grace is sufficient for you"* (2 Corinthians 12:9).

We are also told to come and ask for grace in the time of need. What need? Any need that requires extra help.

*"Let us therefore come boldly to the throne of grace, that we may obtain mercy and find **grace to help in time of need**"* (Hebrews 4:16).

We can see from this scripture that grace helps us in times of need. Grace empowers us to do what we cannot do in our own strength.

We need grace to serve God acceptably

Isn't it good that the Lord will supply us with grace so that we can serve Him acceptably?

"*Therefore, since we are receiving a kingdom which cannot be shaken, let us have grace, by which we [l]may serve God acceptably with reverence and godly fear. 29 For our God is a consuming fire*" (Hebrews 12:28-29).

Our words should minister grace to others

When we speak, we need to ask ourselves: Are these words ministering grace?

"Let your speech always be with grace, seasoned with salt, that you may know how you ought to answer each one" (Colossians 4:6).

When we share the gospel of Christ, we need to do so with grace. People need to know that the price has already been paid. All they need to do is accept the sacrifice of Jesus by confessing with their mouths the Lord Jesus and believing in their hearts that God raised Jesus from the dead (Romans 10:10). This is the gospel message; this is the grace of God.

We need to present the gospel to others in a simple way.

We also need to ensure that our words do not harm others.

"Let no corrupt word proceed out of your mouth, but what is good for necessary [h]edification, that it may impart grace to the hearers" (Ephesians 4:29).

The grace of God empowers us. Our words need to empower others. Whatever they are going through, our words need to encourage and edify others.

Yes, there are times when we have to be blunt and tell people the way things are, which sometimes can be hard but is still the truth. However, within the content of this book, we are speaking about grace.

Grace for giving

Paul was testifying about the grace of giving in the churches of Macedonia (2 Corinthians 8:1-5) and that they should abound in it also.

"But as you abound in everything—in faith, in speech, in knowledge, in all diligence, and in your love for us—see that you abound in this grace also (2 Corinthians 8:7).

This scripture shows us clearly that there is a grace for giving.

We need to be able to identify the grace upon our lives

As has been stated earlier in the book, it is important that we recognise what we are graced for, especially in ministry. As we have said before, grace comes from the Lord. And while we can step in and help occasionally in a place that we are not necessarily called into (provided we are not led otherwise) on a long-term basis, we do need to stay in our grace when it comes to ministry.

"According to the grace of God which was given to me, as a wise master builder I have laid the foundation, and another builds on it. But let each one take heed how he builds on it" (1 Corinthians 3:10).

Chapter 4
How to Grow in Grace

S o, how do we grow in grace?

The scriptures tell us to "grow in grace":

"But grow in the grace and knowledge of our Lord and Savior Jesus Christ" (2 Peter 3:18).

The first step is to actually realise that we do have grace. We must acknowledge the grace that we already have.

We have been given grace by Jesus Christ.

"I thank my God always concerning you for the grace of God which was given to you by Christ Jesus" (1 Corinthians 1:4).

The scriptures also tell us that we have been given grace according to the gift of the measure of Christ (Ephesians 4:7).

Now that we know that we already have grace, how do we grow in the practical application of grace in our lives?

The scriptures tell us how to grow in grace. We are told in the Bible that grace and peace will be multiplied for us through the knowledge of God and the Father.

"Grace and peace be multiplied unto you through the knowledge of God, and of Jesus our Lord" (2 Peter 1:2).

The more knowledge we have of God and of Jesus Christ, the more grace and peace we will have. Notice that it says "multiplied", not added. In practical terms, if we know that God will never fail us, whatever we go through, we will be at peace. This also allows God's grace to be multiplied unto us. Can we see why everyone has to be a student of God's Word?

The knowledge of God and of Jesus Christ can only come through the word of God and by the Holy Spirit revealing to us who the Father is and who Jesus Christ is. This will multiply grace and peace unto us.

Sometimes, we hear of great trials that some people pass through, and we wonder how they can be at such peace. How do they continue to do the things assigned to them? This is one secret: they are walking in greater dimensions of grace and peace than the average believer in Christ. Knowing God and the Lord Jesus Christ better can only work for our own advantage.

The Lord gives grace to the humble (James 4:6), and we can also ask for grace (Hebrews 4:16), but the way that grace and peace are multiplied unto us is through the knowledge of God and of our Lord Jesus Christ (2 Peter 1:2).

Therefore, as we grow in the knowledge of God and of our Lord Jesus Christ, we will have more capacity to do things we struggled to do before because grace empowers. We would also have more capacity to walk in peace and experience the peace of God.

Chapter 5

Our Response to the Grace of God

S o, now that we know that we have been given grace through our Lord Jesus Christ and that we can grow in grace, what should be our response to grace?

The first thing we must realise is that whatever we have is by the grace of God. This is why we should not boast. Our salvation is also by the grace of God (Ephesians 2:8-9).

When the Lord works through us, we must remember that it is the grace of God (1 Corinthians 15:10).

The scriptures also tell us not to frustrate the grace of God. How can a person frustrate the grace of God? By insisting on doing things in our own strength. Salvation is by the grace of God. The Lord has made provision for our salvation through the sacrifice of Jesus. All we need to do is receive this by faith.

We are told not to frustrate the grace of God (Galatians 2:21).

Are you struggling with sin? Then just ask the Lord for grace and stop striving. The scriptures tell us that sin shall not have dominion over us because we are under grace (Romans 6:14).

We are also to be good stewards of the manifold grace of God. We should also know that someone needs the gift the Lord has given to us. We are to be faithful with different expressions of the grace of God.

Neither are we to compare ourselves with others. One person can have grace for business, and another person can have grace for music. We are simply to abide where we have been called (1 Corinthians 7:20).

An understanding of this will really help us. We must remember that grace comes from God. A title must be accompanied by the corresponding grace; otherwise, a person will struggle in such a position.

And let us not forget that the Lord expects us to grow in grace.

The scriptures also tell us to be strong in the grace that is in Christ Jesus (2 Timothy 2:1).

So, what does that look like? We are not supposed to strive after yielding to the Lord's grace. We can also be partakers of another person's grace by association (Philippians 1:7). We will find out that a person who attends or listens to a ministry that is strong in prayer will, after a while, start praying more. The person is drawing from the grace upon that person or ministry.

A fellow Christian author had an event a few years ago, and I went to support her. This lady is very good at writing poems. To my amazement, after the event, I found that I was able to write poems. That is a good example of being a partaker of another person's grace.

Chapter 6
Conclusion

The grace of God is so important that we must acknowledge it to ensure that we do not struggle unnecessarily in our Christian walk.

We have found out that grace and truth came through Jesus Christ our Lord (John 1:17).

Most of the epistles start by saying, *"Grace and peace be unto you"*, and they also end with *"grace be unto you"*.

Here are some few books in the New Testament starting with the word, "grace".

Grace to you, and peace, from God our Father, and the Lord Jesus Christ (1 Corinthians 1:3).

Grace to you and peace from God the Father, and our Lord Jesus Christ (Galatians 1:3).

Grace to you and peace, from God our Father, and the Lord Jesus Christ.

Below are some New Testament books showing them ending with the word "grace".

All who are with me greet you. Greet those who love us in the faith. **Grace** *be with you all. Amen* (Titus 3:15).

The **grace** *of our Lord Jesus Christ be with your spirit. Amen* (Philemon 1:25).

The **grace** *of our Lord Jesus Christ be with you all. Amen* (Revelation 22:21).

The truth is that grace is available for us in all areas of life. The scripture tells us that God is the God of all grace (1 Peter 5:10).

The Lord empowers us by His grace. Let us walk in awareness of this grace in all areas of our lives.

Salvation Prayer

Father God, I come to you in Jesus' name. I admit that I am a sinner, and I now receive the sacrifice that Jesus Christ paid for me.

I confess with my mouth the Lord Jesus, and I believe in my heart that God raised Him from the dead.

I now declare that Jesus Christ is my Lord and Saviour.

Thank you, Father, for saving me in Jesus' name.

I am now your child. Amen.

If you've said this prayer for the first time, send an email to Bisiwrite r@gmail.com . Start reading your Bible and ask the Lord to guide you to a good church.

About the author

Bisi Oladipupo has been a Christian for many years and lives in the United Kingdom with her family.

She has attended a few Bible colleges, and she has completed a diploma in Biblical Studies from a UK Bible college. She has also obtained an associate degree in Bible and Theology from a USA School of Ministry.

She is a teacher of God's Word, coordinates Bible studies, and a Christian fellowship.

Her author page is www.bisiwriter.com

She writes regularly, and her blog website is www.inspiredwords.org

You can contact Bisi by email at bisiwriter@gmail.com

Also by

The Twelve Apostles of Jesus Christ: Lessons We Can Learn

The Lord's Cup in Communion: The Significance of taking the Lord's Supper

Different Ways to Receive Healing from Scripture and Walk in Health

Believing on The Name of Jesus Christ: What Every Believer Needs to Know

The Mind and Your Christian Walk: The Impact of the mind on our Christian walk

Relationship Skills in the Bible: Scriptural Principles of relating to others

The Nature of God's Kingdom: The Characteristics of the Kingdom of God

The Person of the Holy Spirit

41 Insights from the Book of Revelation

The Importance of Spiritual Discernment

God Speaks Through Nature

It's All About the Heart

A Better Covenant: A Look at the Covenants of God and Our Better Covenant

40 Day New Covenant Devotional

What Happens When We Pray ?

Daily Bread for Healing: A 40-day Healing Devotional

40 Facts of Who Jesus Is: A Devotional

50 Prayers for Your Children and Generations to Come

Afterword

If you enjoyed this book, please take a few moments to write a review of it online at the store where it was purchased. Thank you

Printed in Great Britain
by Amazon